THE HOW AND WHY WONDER BOOK OF
ANTS AND BEES

Written by
RONALD N. ROOD

Illustrated by
CYNTHIA ILIFF KOEHLER
and ALVIN KOEHLER

Editorial Production:
DONALD D. WOLF

Edited under the supervision of
Dr. Paul E. Blackwood
Washington, D. C.

Text and illustrations approved by
Oakes A. White
Brooklyn Children's Museum
Brooklyn, New York

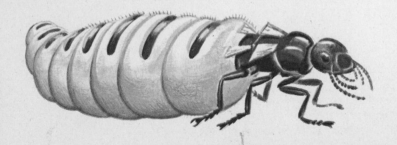

WONDER BOOKS · NEW YORK
A Division of GROSSET & DUNLAP, Inc.

Introduction

Anyone who doubts that truth is stranger than fiction need only study the habits of the social insects to have his opinion changed. For the life patterns of these six-legged animals reveal events of sheer wonder that could scarcely be imagined by the best fiction writer.

Scientists have studied the social insects for centuries, and a fairly complete picture of the peculiar and fascinating behavior of these insects is available. This *How and Why Wonder Book* accurately presents the essential characteristics of the four families of social insects — bees, wasps, ants and termites.

To a casual observer, many of the actions of social insects may appear strange. Are dancing bees really dancing? Are bumblebees being mischievous when they walk up to an intruder and plaster it with a gluey mess of honey? Whatever the appearance of such actions to a casual observer, close study shows that they are important to the insects in building and maintaining their insect society.

It is possible for anyone to watch social insects at close range. This can be done at home or in school by making an observation nest. Directions for making one are found in this book. Such a project is fun as well as instructive for individuals or class groups.

The study of social insects is a part of the science course in many schools. For this reason, *The How and Why Wonder Book of Ants and Bees* will be a useful addition to both home and school libraries.

Paul E. Blackwood

Dr. Blackwood is a professional employee in the U. S. Office of Education. This book was edited by him in his private capacity and no official support or endorsement by the Office of Education is intended or should be inferred.

Library of Congress Catalog Card Number: 62-9677

© 1962, by Wonder Books, Inc.
All rights reserved under International and Pan-American Copyright Conventions.
Published simultaneously in Canada.   Printed in the United States of America.

Contents

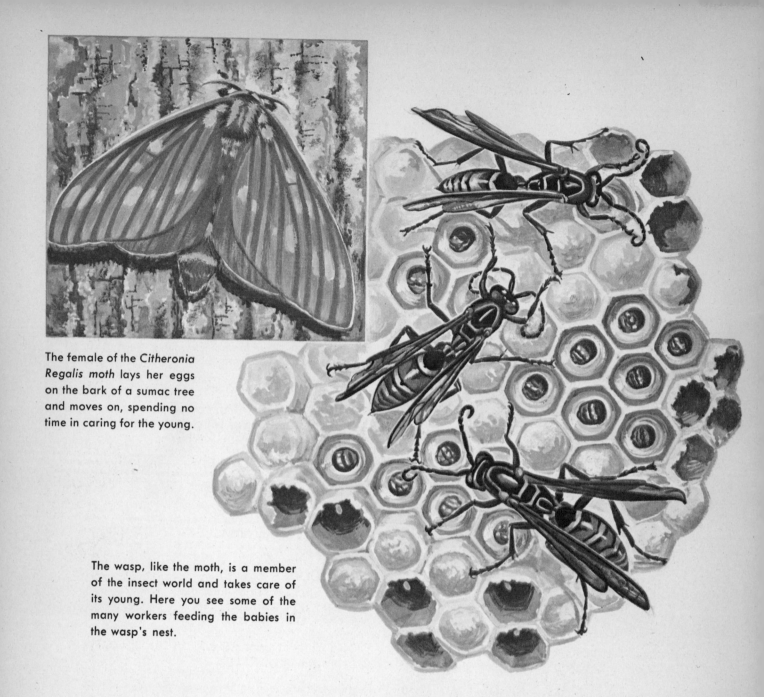

The female of the *Citheronia Regalis* moth lays her eggs on the bark of a sumac tree and moves on, spending no time in caring for the young.

The wasp, like the moth, is a member of the insect world and takes care of its young. Here you see some of the many workers feeding the babies in the wasp's nest.

SOCIAL INSECTS

The female moth creeps slowly along a tree limb. Finally she stops and lays a few eggs. They stick to the bark. Then she crawls away.

When her babies hatch, they must make their way by themselves. There are no parents to protect them. Alone, they must find food and hide from their enemies.

Most other insects do the same thing. The mosquito sets her eggs afloat on a little raft. Walking-stick insects just drop theirs on the ground. Other insects place their eggs where their young may find food and shelter. Then they leave them forever.

How strange it is, then, to see a wasp caring for her babies! She brings food, chews it up until it is soft and places it in their little mouths. She licks them, strokes them with her antennae, or "feelers," and builds a shelter to keep out the sun and the rain. If danger strikes, she flies toward it, even if it is an animal a thousand times her size.

Of all the insects, only bees, wasps, ants and termites take care of their families. The family, in turn, helps the mother to care for her later offspring. Because of this, and also because these insects live in little groups or societies, they are called "social insects."

Nobody is sure how the social habit developed. But scientists have noticed an interesting thing. Often, as soon as the young insects are given food, they produce little bubbles of saliva. The

Ants, like bees, are social insects. The fire ants above carry a larva and a cocoon to a safer place. Below are two termites licking each other. This is a process that, according to scientists, helps to keep the insect family together.

A bee will defend the hive against a larger enemy.

adult insects lick up the saliva quickly. Then the adults produce more saliva, which other adult insects lick up.

Does this special substance in the bubbles help to keep the insect family together? Many scientists think so. They call the process *trophallaxis* or "nursing together." As one scientist said, "To others in the nest, each insect must be a living lollipop."

What kinds of homes do these insects have in their hollow trees and paper nests? What happens after they have gone through the entrance hole and disappeared from sight? This book helps to tell their wonderful story.

A worker bee on a honeycomb.

(actual size)

The Castle of Wax

The honeybees come from every direction. Each one finds the target — an opening only an inch wide. Out of this opening stream other honeybees, circling for a moment before they dart away. The wax castle of the bees is humming with life.

Inside the opening is an amazing scene.

What is inside the wax castle? No factory ever ran with more bustle and activity. Hanging from the roof are heavy curtains of wax. They may be larger than this book and four times as thick. On both sides of the curtains are countless honeybees, poking their heads into hundreds of little cells or chambers.

This is the castle of ten thousand rooms.

How many rooms does it have? Each cell of the curtains is a little room by itself. Although we often speak of the curtains as "honeycomb," a great many of them do not contain honey at all. The cells of the brood comb each have a small inhabitant — a grublike larva that will soon turn into a new honeybee. For the larva, the cell is a cradle, living room and bedroom combined. The larva stays in it from the day it hatches until the day it is fully grown.

Nurse bees are walking all over the brood comb. Some-

What do the nurse bees do? times they put their feet right on the heads of the babies. One after the other, they bend down and poke their heads inside the cells. They feed and lick their little sisters in their cradles.

There is another kind of cell on the edge of the comb. It is much larger than the others. It looks almost like a peanut shell made out of wax. Inside it is a larva just like the thousands of others — only a little larger. This strange cell must be something special to be off on the side of the comb where it can have plenty of room. Indeed it is, for it is the royal nursery of the larva that will soon become the new queen.

Over on the true "honeycomb," some-

Why do bees evaporate their honey? thing strange is taking place. Bees are walking slowly over the half-filled cells, beating their wings as if they were trying to fly. As the breeze from their wings fans across the cells, it makes the sweet liquid evaporate. A cell that was filled with honey may be only three-quarters full the next day as a result of the air from their wings. This seems like a waste — to bring in nectar from the flowers and then evaporate it so there is not much left. But one taste of the liquid will tell why it is done. The sugar that stays behind as the water evaporates gets thicker and sweeter.

The wild beehive in a hollow tree clearly shows the various combs, hanging down like curtains and drapes in a home.

QUEEN

DRONE

WORKER

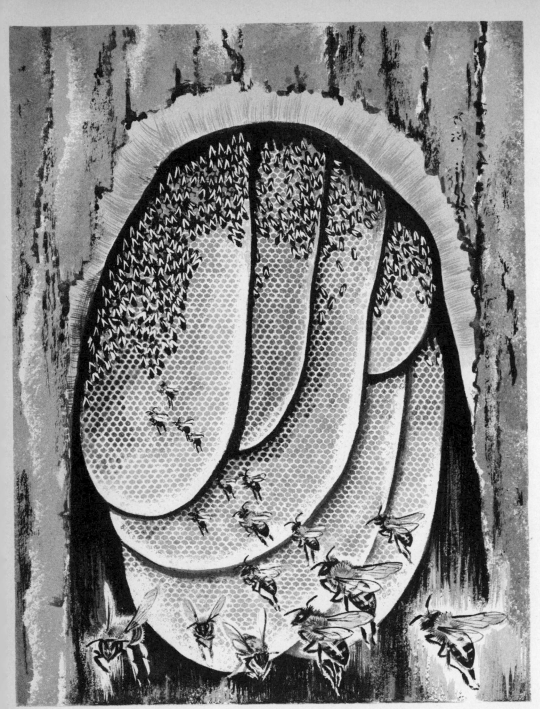

There are "pantry cells," too, for storage of pollen as food. But in another part of the hive is a comb that seems deserted. Each of the cells has been covered with a wax cap. They hang heavy and still, as if they have been forgotten. But they are filled with golden treasure — the nectar brought from the fields and changed in the bodies of the bees into thick, rich honey. Each pound of it is the work of many bees. Sometimes

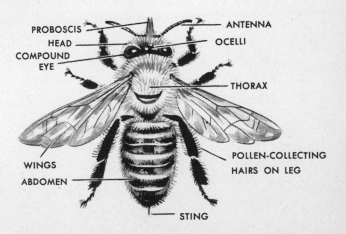

PROBOSCIS
HEAD
COMPOUND EYE
ANTENNA
OCELLI
THORAX
POLLEN-COLLECTING HAIRS ON LEG
WINGS
ABDOMEN
STING

The form, structure and vital parts of a bee (worker).

The building of queen cells gets special attention. They are larger than the other cells and are built at the edge of the comb so that they get more air. Some of the cells above are under construction. The one at the right is ready to receive an egg.

A living fan to condition air and condense honey.

work without being told. There are enough workers of each kind — nurses, honey-fanners, pollen-gatherers and wax-makers. If the hive gets too hot, some of the bees set up an air current with their wings as a ventilation system. If more wax is needed, extra bees set about making it.

Suddenly one bee appears that looks different from the others.

What is the job of the drone bee?

Its head seems to be completely covered with two huge eyes, like a helmet. Its legs are shaped differently; its body is longer. It walks up to a worker bee and seems to ask for food. The worker stops work and gives it a bit of honey. Then it goes to another for more food, and so on. How strange to see this kind of bee in a bustling hive where all the others are working!

Yet this bee has a job, too. It is one of the most important of the bees. It is a drone, or male bee, one of a few dozen brothers among the thousands of worker sisters. Its job will begin when that peanut-shaped queen cell has opened and the new queen has made her

they have to make more than thirty-five thousand trips into the fields to produce a single pound of honey.

There may be thirty thousand bees in the hive, and each one has a job to do. There are no loafers. There are no supervisors to see that all are working. Every bee does its

How many bees live in a hive?

If there is not enough food available, a worker might evict a drone from the hive.

The drone, unable to eat by itself, is fed by workers or it starves.

way into the world. For it must provide millions of tiny sperm cells that the queen bee stores in a special pouch in her body. Then, just before she places new eggs in the brood comb, she fertilizes each one with a sperm cell, so that it can develop into a new worker.

Once it was thought that the drones were lazy because they didn't help with the hive duties. But now we know that they couldn't help, no matter how much they wanted to. Their legs, heads and bodies are not shaped right for fashioning the wax into the perfect little chambers. They don't even have a sting with which they can help to drive away enemies. They just have those important little sperm cells, ready to be given to the queen in mating.

The "song of the hive" is a steady, high-pitched hum. It

What causes the "song of the hive"? is made by the wings of the bees as they go about their work. Suddenly the song becomes louder. Then scratchings and squeaking can be heard. A mouse has tried to steal the honey. But the bees are always on their guard. They

attack the mouse and drive it away from their nest.

Sometimes their attack is so fierce that they kill the mouse. Then they have a real problem. It's almost like having a dead elephant in the living room. If they don't do something quickly, the odor of the mouse will spoil the honey. But how can they get such a big creature out of the hive?

The answer lies in another kind of

How do bees keep their hive clean? building material used by bees—*propolis* or "bee-glue." Quickly they get the sticky material from certain buds and twigs.

Then they work it into a liquid which they use to cover the dead mouse. When it dries, it looks like tough brown paint. The mouse is sealed in its own little tomb, right inside the hive.

This is just one method of garbage disposal. The bees keep their hive clean at all times. Anything that doesn't belong there gets dumped outside. Sometimes a worker will drag out a protesting drone as if he were a piece of rubbish. Then the drone crawls back in again, and five minutes later the same worker may be giving him some honey.

No one is sure how the bees know what job they are supposed to do. But each one of them, doing its little task, helps the whole hive to operate like a big, humming machine. Sometimes the "machine" is located in a hollow tree. Other times it is in a specially-built beehive. The Bible tells us that Samson found bees in the body of a dead lion. But no matter where their home is located, the bees always build the same wax curtain-combs with the same six-sided cells, half an inch long and a quarter-inch wide.

The cells are so perfect and regular that the French scientist Réaumur once suggested they could be used as a unit of measurement.

How can the honeybee do all her many jobs and make such perfect wax cells? Some of the answers will be found in the next chapter.

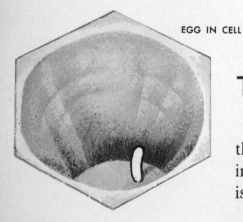

EGG IN CELL

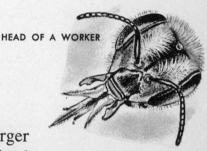

HEAD OF A WORKER

The Magic of Bees

From a blind, helpless baby no larger than a grain of sugar to a full-fledged insect with a whole set of tools — that is the story of the honeybee. It begins

The gray, comma-shaped egg is attached to the bottom of the cell with an adhesive secretion.

A blind and legless grub hatches from the egg. It is fed continuously until it starts spinning a cocoon after a few days.

WORKER FEEDING LARVA

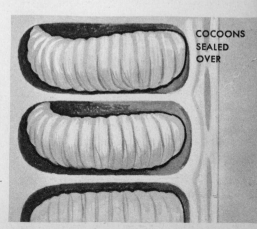

COCOONS SEALED OVER

life as a tiny comma-shaped egg. It can hardly be seen in the cell that seems so huge in comparison. It hatches three days after it is placed there by the queen mother. But it doesn't look like a bee at all. It is just a white, legless, blind grub that seems to be all appetite.

Food is near at hand. A few minutes **How does a new bee get its food?** after the grub has hatched, the head of a full-grown bee appears at the grub's cell. Poking down to the new arrival, the adult bee supplies it with "royal jelly" — a paste made in special glands in the bee's head. No sooner has it fed the little larva and gone on to the next cell than another load of food arrives. Then another comes, and another, and another — about once every minute.

Instead of choking on all this food, the **How does the baby bee grow?** larva begins to swell like a balloon. Its skin gets tighter, like a jacket that is too small. Soon it splits and the grub wriggles free. The next day it molts, or sheds its jacket, again. Finally, the larva has become so large that it fills its cell. It has been fed about ten thousand times — royal jelly

for the first two days and "bee bread," or flower pollen mixed with honey, for four more. Now it is as big as the eraser on the end of a new pencil—more than a thousand times larger than it was a week ago.

It begins to produce a sticky silk from glands near its mouth. Weaving back and forth, it spins the silk into a lacy cocoon. Then it lies still, like a mummy wrapped in cloth.

All over the brood comb, hundreds of other bee larvae are doing the same thing. The queen mother that laid the eggs may have produced a thousand that same day — placing each in its own six-sided cell. Just before the larvae start to form cocoons, the nurse bees seal their rooms with wax. Then they go on to the care of other babies.

Inside the cocoon there is a great change. The soft, legless grub body stiffens. Outlines of legs, wings, eyes, antennae, or "feelers," begin to form. The larva is a larva no longer, but a pupa — darkening, hardening, full of promise of the honeybee to come.

Twelve days later, a sharp new pair of jaws begins to cut away at the wax cap of the cell. Now comes the greatest marvel of all. The cell opens and out comes a clean new honeybee — her

WORKERS (ACTUAL SIZE)

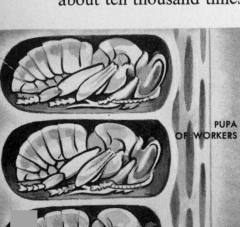

PUPA OF WORKERS

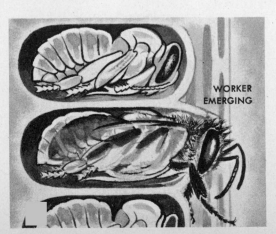

WORKER EMERGING

Here, in the cocoon, the great change takes place: from grub to milk-white nymph or pupa, until one day the adult bee emerges. If the egg is fertilized, the bee will become a worker. If not fertilized, it will become a drone.

The wax can be seen in this close-up view of the underside of a worker bee.

To make wax for building new cells, bees hang in chains from combs. Thin slips of wax come from their abdominal plates as they stretch themselves.

four shining wings thinner than paper, her six legs ready to cling to the petals of the flowers she has never seen. Scientists say that such a change, from a grub to a bee, is as wonderful as putting a truck into a garage, closing the door and taking out a beautiful new airplane twelve days later.

All around her are hundreds of other workers, busy at their tasks. After buzzing her new wings and stretching her new legs for a day or so, she goes to work herself. She feeds pollen and honey to her younger sisters, all ready to build cocoons of

What does a new worker do?

their own. Then in a few days, the glands in her head begin to make royal jelly for the newborn babies. One of them may be growing in the same cell she occupied just a few days before.

New wax is needed for the comb. The young worker takes great drinks of honey and then "hangs herself up" in a sheet of living bodies with her sisters. Each one hangs with her front feet attached to the hind legs of the one above. After a few hours little plates of wax appear on each abdomen. Wax oozes out through special glands. Shaping the wax with the jaws and feet,

How is beeswax made?

the bees build new cells like the thousands already there.

A bee cannot always produce beeswax. Nor can it always produce royal jelly. The life of bees runs in a series of stages. Once the bee has passed a certain point, it does not go back again. Young workers can make royal jelly for a few days. Then they can make wax. Then, when they are older, they go out into the fields to gather nectar and pollen. So if we know what kind of work a bee is doing, we have some idea of how old it is.

When she leaves the hive, the worker is almost like a puppy in a strange new yard. She flies around and around, never straying far from the hive. Her great compound eyes take in the form of rocks and trees nearby. The six thousand "smell-plates" on her antennae receive strange odors from the new world, but she doesn't venture away until a day or two later. Then she begins the job that will last the rest of her life.

BEE
(ACTUAL SIZE)

She carries her tool kit right with her.

What is the bee's tool kit? It is in the form of bristles and spines on her legs. She has a pair of "pollen baskets" on her hind legs to stuff full of the golden powder from flowers. Her front legs have cleaning brushes for the delicate antennae. Spines on the middle legs help pry pollen out of the pollen baskets. Other spines help her trim and shape the wax for the comb.

When she goes from one flower to another, she pokes her head deep into its center to get the sweet nectar. Hairs on her body brush the powdery pollen around. She stuffs it in her pollen baskets. Then some of it rubs off as she brushes around in the next flower.

The bees collect pollen on their hind legs. Pollen is held in place by long leg hairs, which form the so-called "pollen baskets" (right).

With its long proboscis, the bee sucks the nectar that is produced in the bottom of the flower. In doing so, the bee pollinates the flower, making it possible to produce seeds (below).

EMPTY
POLLEN BASKET

FILLED POLLEN BASKET

The more circles a bee "dances," the farther away are flowers with nectar.

Mixed from flower to flower, pollen is needed for blossoms to develop their fruit and seeds. The seeds can grow into new plants. If the bees didn't scatter the pollen, there would probably be no orchards. Apples, peaches, strawberries, oranges and other fruit would be unknown. There would be no pretty flowers in the garden. The honey produced by bees in the United States alone is worth about a hundred million dollars each year. This, however, is small compared to the value of all the fruit and flowers.

Why do farmers like the bees?

Why doesn't the pollen from a dandelion get mixed with the flower from a rose? Simply because the honeybee visits only one kind of flower at a time. She may fly over a whole field of dandelions to get to a rose garden. The next day, she may visit nothing but clover.

An apple tree begins to unfold its flowers early one May morning. By eight o'clock, hundreds of fragrant pink-and-white blooms have opened. A single bee discovers them. She takes nectar from a few blossoms. Then she stuffs her baskets with pollen, circles around for a few seconds and is gone. In less than half an hour the tree is buzzing with dozens of honeybees. How did she tell them about her wonderful find of a tree full of flowers?

The answer was found by Dr. Karl von Frisch of Germany, when he discovered the "dancing bees." When the worker returned from the apple tree, she began to do a little dance near the entrance to the hive. First she circled one way, then another. In between the circles she walked a little straight line, wiggling like an excited puppy. Soon the others followed her in her dance, doing just the same as she was doing. The circles tell how far away the flowers are — the more circles, the farther away. The straight line tells the direction to travel, and the odor of the flowers still clinging to her body tells them what kind of flowers they will find. In a few minutes they fly away, one after another — right to the apple tree!

What are the "dancing bees"?

Every worker is a little chemistry laboratory. When she stuffs herself full of nectar, she stores it in a little pouch in her abdomen, the "honey stomach." There it is changed in a process

How is honey made?

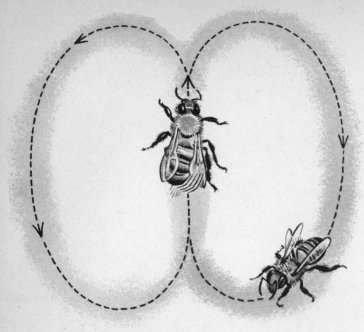

The straight line in the bee's dance shows the direction of the flower. The tail-wagging gives the scent.

sends it down. Ultraviolet light, too — the same invisible rays that cause a sunburn — guides the bees. And their huge compound eyes make out the shape of familiar trees and houses. They find their way by the colors of flowers, too — all but one color. The bees are color-blind to red.

that is still a mystery. Somehow it becomes thin honey, which is like nothing else on earth. Man has tried for years to learn to make honey out of sweetened water or even the nectar of flowers. But so far he has been defeated. Whether honey is in a honeycomb, in jars on a supermarket shelf, in cough syrup or spread on a slice of bread, every drop of it has been made by honeybees.

Beekeepers know that bees find their way by means of the sun. But what do they do on a cloudy day? They can still sense where the sun is in the sky by means of polarized light. This is light that can be seen better from one direction than from others. Even behind the clouds, the sun still

How do bees find their way?

HONEY STOMACH   INTESTINE

WAX

Honey is produced in the intestinal tract of the bee. Man has not been able to make artificial honey.

Day after day the bee travels back and forth. Little hooks between her wings hold them together for strength in flight. The wings buzz as much as two hundred times per second. But in a few days they begin to get frayed on the edges. In a couple of weeks they are slightly torn. A little more than a month from the time she first spread their shining beauty in the sun, the faithful wings are tattered.

How long do bees live?

She works with them until she can fly no longer. One day she finds her load of pollen and nectar too heavy. The bee drops to the ground, half-crawling, half-flying toward the hive. There, six or eight weeks after she visited her first flower, her days of work come to an end.

She may give her life in another way, too. If an enemy strikes, she flies to the attack. She drives her sting deep into its flesh. But as she pulls away the little

Why does a bee die when it stings?

barbs on the sting hold fast. It is pulled out of her body, leaving her torn and dying. Although a bee sting means pain for the victim, it means death for the honeybee.

No matter what happens to the workers, life in the hive goes on. The new babies receive their two days of royal jelly followed by pollen and honey. But the larva in the queen cell continues to get royal jelly every day. This makes a wonderful change. Instead of a regular-sized worker, unable to lay eggs, the diet of royal jelly will produce a sleek new queen.

Even though the queen has not yet left her cocoon, a strange sound is coming from her cell. It can be heard above the song of the hive.

A new princess is about to be born.

A queen honeybee emerges from the irregular wax cell in which she has developed.

The Captive Queen

The new queen is one third larger than **What does the new queen look like?** the workers. Her legs lack their tools and combs. Her wings are folded and damp against her body, but they are vibrating with a high-pitched hum that pierces the walls of the hive. Quickly she bites at the top of her cocoon and the cap of her queen cell.

At last she is free. Scarcely waiting for her wings to dry, she rushes over the brood comb. The workers make way for her. Finally, she finds what she is seeking. Another queen cell is waiting. From it, too, comes the strange song. The workers stand by as she tears at the cap until she has opened it. Then she thrusts her sting deep, again and again. Unlike the workers, she can use her long, curved sting many times. But she uses it only against other queens.

If two queens emerge from cocoons at the same instant, there is a duel. The insects thrust at each other with their sharp stings until only one of the queens is left alive.

She can no more stop from stinging her **Why does she kill her sister queens?** sister queens than the workers can stop gathering in the fields. "One queen per hive" is the rule that she must follow. She may have six or eight other queens seeking to destroy her if she allows them to live. Only after she has made sure that she is the only queen bee in the hive does she finally stop to rest.

QUEEN BEE
(ACTUAL SIZE)

"One queen per hive" is the rule she must follow. If two queens emerge from their cocoons at the same instant, a battle to the death develops. Here two queens duel it out.

If there is only a single queen for each hive, what will happen when she meets her queen mother? To find the answer we have to go back a few days. The queen mother put a normal egg into each special cell as she came to it. Fed only royal jelly by the workers, each one developed into a queen larva. Then, as the time came near for their emergence as new queens, a change came over the entire hive.

What happens to the old queen mother?

Gone is the old need to spend every moment working in the fields. Even the queen mother's constant job of laying eggs is forgotten. Tearing open the caps of the honeycomb, thousands of bees drink so deeply that they become stuffed. This is probably a wise provision by nature for the time ahead. For this is known as the time of the swarm.

The queen mother and several thousand of her family will leave the hive forever to find a new home.

The workers are so full that some of them can hardly fly. Many, like the fat man who couldn't bend over to tie his own shoe, are unable to curve their abdomens enough to use their stings. In fact, they seem too good-natured to sting. The song of the hive rises to a new pitch. Everything is in preparation for a great adventure.

Finally the great day comes. The sun is shining and the weather is fair—the beekeepers call it a "swarm day." The bees fly out by the hundreds and thousands. Away they go to a nearby tree or bush where they cluster in a close mass. The ones on the outside of the mass open little scent-

What is a "swarm day"?

Bees are easily irritated, but they will often allow themselves to be handled this way on swarm days.

hollow tree or empty hive. The swarm follows them to the new home.

Sometimes the beekeeper wishes to find the queen. Then he may shake the swarm into a tub of water. As the bees begin to swim toward the sides, he can usually find her by her large size. Occasionally, he discovers that the bees have swarmed without her. This is like having a birthday party for someone who didn't get invited. The swarm cannot live more than a few days without its queen. Only she can lay the eggs to produce new workers.

How is the queen like a prisoner?

The queen, whether it is the new queen back in the hive, or the queen mother in the swarm, is not really a ruler. She is more like a prisoner than a queen. She must be fed and cared for by her workers. Except for her swarming and mating flights, she never sees the outside world.

The old queen has left. Now the new queen pushes toward the opening of the

glands on their abdomen and fan the scent out into the air with their wings. They do this to guide others to the spot, just as they often do when they find a rich source of nectar or a cluster of flowers.

The clustered swarm is thick and heavy. It can often be shaken from the bush into an empty hive like a huge bunch of overripe grapes. Somewhere in the center of the swarm is the queen mother. Soon some bees have found a

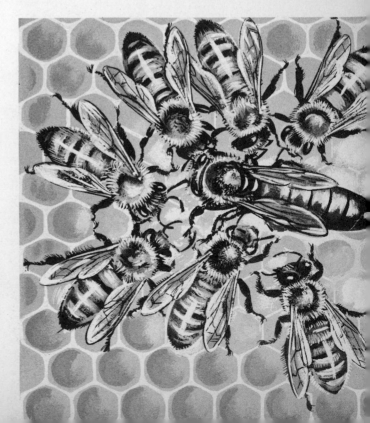

hive. A most important job waits for her. At last the drones will get a chance to do their part. She takes off on her new wings, circling around and around. The drones follow. Sometimes she goes out of sight.

Finally she mates with one of the drones. She may **What happens to the drones after mating?** choose one from another hive as far as nine miles away. The millions of tiny sperm cells from the drone's body are placed in a pouch in the queen's abdomen. His work done at last, the drone soon dies. The other drones are driven from the hive when the food supply gets low in the fall.

Back in the hive, she becomes the new queen mother. Day **How many eggs does the new queen produce?** after day she lays thousands of eggs —often four or five thousand a day. Such egg production is a great task. So she is fed by the work-

ers almost constantly. They feed her and lick her, caring for her every need.

Perhaps this licking and passing around material from her **What happens if the queen is taken away?** body serves to keep the hive going smoothly. If the queen is taken away or dies, the workers create a new queen by enlarging a cell and keeping one of the newborn babies on a steady royal jelly diet. If this doesn't work, the workers themselves manage to lay a few eggs, but these develop only into drones. Then the hive, without a queen, soon dies.

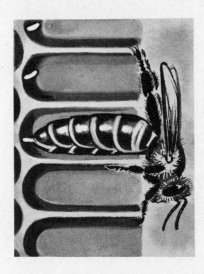

A queen laying eggs.

If nothing happens to the queen, she may live with her **How long does the queen live?** huge family for four or five years. During this time she may lay a million eggs. What a difference between the queen mother and the single moth who leaves a few eggs on a twig in the fall!

But there are many other bees, too. They live in interesting places — old mouse nests, hollow chunks of wood, even tin cans. Their story will be told in the next chapter.

Attendants constantly surround the queen. When she pauses in her egg-laying, they clean and feed her.

Bees Without a Hive

A bee that doesn't sting! It is hard to believe, but there are bees in South America that never sting at all. They live in colonies, or large families, just like the honeybees. Instead of living in a man-made hive, they make their homes in hollow trees or caves. Here they build combs out of wax and clay or from the sticky resin of trees.

Since they don't sting, they have a different way of protecting their little honeypots and the larvae in the cells. When an enemy comes, they fly all over it, biting and scratching. Strong fluid from their mouths and bodies causes a burning sensation. It feels almost like spattering grease. But even so, South American natives often keep them in little "drums." These are made of a hollow log with both ends sealed, except

How do stingless bees fight enemies?

for a little hole for the bees to enter. When the natives want some honey, they just break open the end of a drum.

Often this honey is delicious. But sometimes it is not. The stingless bees visit all kinds of flowers. If there aren't enough flowers available, they take the next best thing. This may be a molasses can or an old grapefruit peel, with a drop or two of motor oil for variety. A South American meal with native honey must be full of surprises!

The honeybee and the stingless bees take care of the eggs laid by the queen. But many of the other kinds of queens take care of their own eggs. One of the strangest is the queen bumblebee. She sits on her eggs in the spring

How is a queen bumblebee like a mother bird?

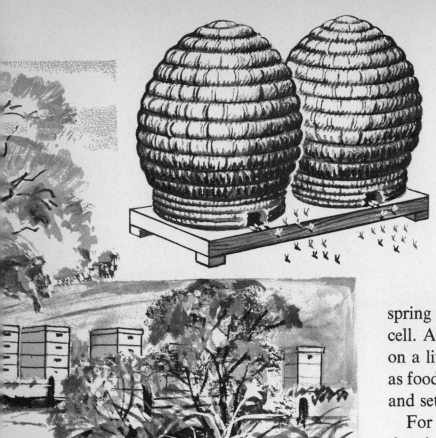

An apiary (a place where bees are kept) set in a landscape with fruit trees is always an interesting sight. The large "boxes" are actually modern beehives. They have replaced the less practical straw skeps (inset at right) that were used for a long time throughout the whole world. The movable frames of the modern hive (cross section on page 20) is much more convenient for the beekeeper and for the bees as well. The queen and the young can get only to section "B," leaving the honey in the top combs undisturbed for the keeper.

like a little bird. All winter long she remains in a sheltered spot, hidden from the cold and storm. When spring comes at last, she goes house-hunting. She flies over the meadow, looking for a little hollow in the ground. Sometimes she even uses an old mouse nest or a half-hidden tin can.

She makes two wax cells. One of them is her honeypot. She fills it with honey she has made from the early spring flowers. The other is her brood cell. About eight eggs go into it, often on a little pad of pollen that will serve as food. Then she caps it over with wax and settles down on top of it.

For the queen bumblebee, babysitting is no problem. When the larvae hatch in three or four days, she opens their cell to feed them. But when they are fed, she closes it up again. She may do this several times a day, flying away for more food in between.

Close-up of the head of a stingless bee and the log shed in which Mexican Indians of Yucatán keep them.

A queen bumblebee helps the young workers out of their cells. Creeping to the honeypots, they help themselves.

LARVAE IN SHELLS

COCOONS

Only the bumblebee, which can reach the nectar, is able to pollinate red clover.

What are the bumblebee's enemies? When she leaves home, she may get into all kinds of trouble. Some kinds of birds like to eat bumblebees — sting and all. A huge robber fly, looking like a bumblebee itself, may lie waiting in a flower, ready to catch her. Sometimes she comes across the nest of another bumblebee. In she goes, just as if it were her own home. She may even drive out the rightful queen and settle down on the eggs herself. This is hard on the babies back at her own home. Sometimes the homeless queen finds the unoccupied nest and begins to take care of it. Thus the two "mothers" have switched nests. More often, an unprotected nest is found by a mouse that helps itself to the tender baby bees and honey.

What are "callows"? The queen helps the new workers, called "callows," out of their cells. Now they are about three weeks old. They are wet and silver-looking at first — hardly like the fuzzy black and yellow queen. Creeping to the honeypot, they help themselves. In a day or two, they are flying over the fields. Sometimes they are caught in a shower, but they just go inside a hanging flower. It shelters them like a sweet-scented umbrella.

Bumblebees seldom sting. They are peaceful, hard-working creatures, but they can sting again and again when necessary. They attack by clawing, biting and scratching. Although there may be only a few hundred bumblebees in a colony, with only fifteen or twenty at home at a time, few creatures make an effort to steal the honey from the little waxen pots.

How is honey used by bees for defense? Strange as it seems, even the honey is used for defense by some kinds of bumblebees. If an enemy attacks, a bumblebee quietly walks up to it, a drop of honey on its tongue. Then the bee plasters the intruder with the gluey stuff. Messy and dripping, the enemy retreats as fast as its sticky feet will let it.

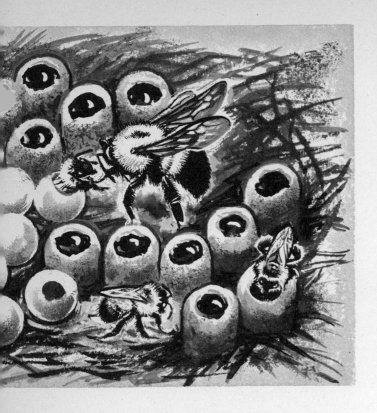

care for themselves. Finally, when they are ready to emerge, each one bites through the hard walls of its home and comes into the world.

Sometimes African explorers come across the ruins of an ancient city. The walls are covered with the hard plaster of the mason bees. The explorers chip away at it, scraping carefully. Sometimes, after they have removed it, they come to nothing but a blank wall. Other times, they come to ancient writings or stone-pictures. These important findings have been hidden for many centuries by the work of these little cement-makers, the mason bees.

What is a carpenter bee?

The jaws of the carpenter bee are strong little tools. The bee itself looks like a bumblebee, but makes its home in wood. Hollowing out a tunnel in a beam or board with its jaws, it builds a little chamber for its eggs. Sometimes these tunnels may twist and turn through lumber for eight or ten feet. Some carpenter bees save themselves a lot of work. They build their nests in hollow bamboo stems. Thus the tunnel is already made for them to live in.

How do mason bees build their homes?

The jaws of mason bees bite through sand and clay. The mother builds her nest out of mud and fills it with pollen and nectar. The mud hardens until it is like stone. The larvae inside feed and

How many kinds of bees are known?

There are about ten thousand kinds of bees known in the world today. Only a few of them are social kinds living in families. There are "cuckoo" bees that sneak into nests of other bees and lay their eggs. Others steal honey to feed their own young. Burrowing bees make holes in the ground. Sweat bees cling to men and animals in summer, lapping the sweat from their bodies. Leafcutting bees trim slices of leaves that they paste together for their homes.

To tell the stories of all the bees would take many books. But there are many more kinds of social insects. The next chapter will tell about the wonderful world of wasps, regarded as among the most intelligent of insects.

CARPENTER BEE

MASON BEE

BURROWING BEE

LEAFCUTTER NEST   LEAFCUTTING BEE

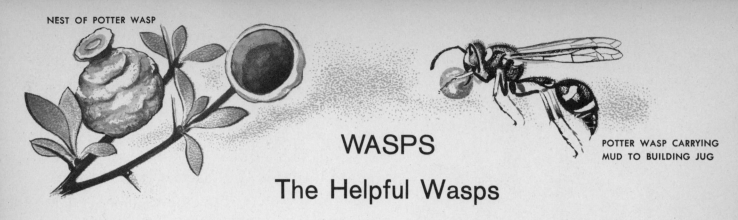

NEST OF POTTER WASP

POTTER WASP CARRYING
MUD TO BUILDING JUG

WASPS

The Helpful Wasps

Nearly everybody likes fig bars. There wouldn't be a single one if it weren't for the tiny fig wasp. She wanders around on the blossom of the fig, spreading the pollen and making it possible for the fruit to develop. Her young hatch out and seek new blossoms. This valuable insect was actually imported into California for the production of Smyrna figs.

What is a fig wasp?

There are about ten thousand kinds of wasps. Only a few of them are social. Most of them live their lives quietly and

How many kinds of wasps are there?

unseen. Some of their relatives, the horntails and sawflies, attack trees and fruit, but a great many of the true wasps are as useful as honeybees.

The tomato hornworm caterpillar is a bad garden pest. It feeds on the leaves of tomato vines and damages the blossoms. A tiny wasp, the

How do wasps help farmers?

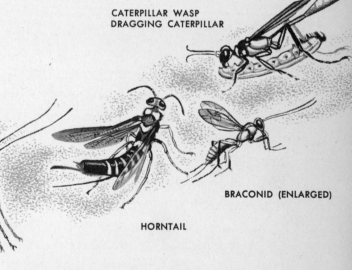

CATERPILLAR WASP
DRAGGING CATERPILLAR

BRACONID (ENLARGED)

HORNTAIL

ICHNEUMON FLY

braconid, pokes her sharp abdomen into the caterpillar several times. Each thrust may release a dozen eggs. The young feed on the pest, finally coming outside to make their little cocoons. The caterpillar soon dies.

Other braconid wasps can produce a whole family with just one egg. This is done when a certain wasp finds the

At left, the nest of a mason wasp; above, the insect itself.

caterpillar of harmful fruit moths or corn borers. Although she is tiny, her amazing egg makes up for her lack of size. After she lays it, it begins to divide into many little cell-groups. Each group produces a hungry larva. It feeds on the body of the caterpillar. Then just as the caterpillar dies, the newborn wasps fly away.

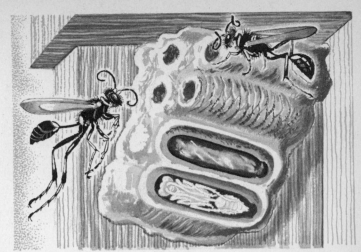

A mud-dauber nest and wasps and two opened cells.

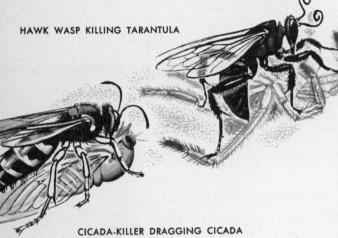

HAWK WASP KILLING TARANTULA

CICADA-KILLER DRAGGING CICADA

A single egg may produce fifty or more wasps. Then if each wasp produces fifty more, there will be twenty-five hundred wasps in a few weeks, all looking for fruit moths.

A huge ichneumon wasp goes flying through the air. It stops at a dying maple tree. Slowly it crawls over the bark, tapping with its antennae. Finally it stops and arches its back. A long thread-like organ, the *ovipositor,* goes to work. Sharp-pointed and strong, it drills deep into the wood.

Why do some wasps drill into trees?

Often people kill this wasp when they see it drilling into a tree. But this is just what shouldn't be done. For the wasp drills until she comes to the tunnel of a wood borer, the real villain. The wasp's larva, hatching out, will destroy the wood borer before it can kill any more trees.

Some wasps are even hitchhikers. One, known as Phanurus, rides around on a moth like a man on a horse. Then, when the moth finally lays its eggs, the little hitchhiker gets off. She lays her own eggs on the moth eggs. Both may start to develop, but it is only the little wasps that hatch out and fly away.

What wasp is a hitchhiker?

The Bible tells of plagues of locusts, which still bother people in many parts of the world. When the female locust lays her eggs underground, the Scelio wasp waits nearby. As fast as the locust buries new eggs, the wasp pokes her ovipositor down into them and lays eggs of her own. The two may work side by side — the locust laying eggs and the wasp destroying them.

25

Hunter wasps catch and paralyze spiders with a carefully-placed sting.

How do hunter wasps feed their young?

Sand wasps do the same with caterpillars. The spider or caterpillar is then placed in the cell of the wasp's nest. Three or four more victims may be added. Then the wasp lays an egg. The new larva has fresh food until it becomes fully grown.

Mud-dauber wasps make many of their homes out of mud, almost like the mason bees. Often they can be seen against the sides of buildings or under roofs. Filled with paralyzed spiders, each cell of the home soon opens to release a new wasp. Potter wasps make little mud jugs and stock them with caterpillars.

How do the wasps catch the spiders? Often a wasp may hang by one leg from the web and sting the spider when it rushes out to catch it. The "tarantula hawk" wasp stings the huge, hairy tarantula and then buries this spider with the wasp egg.

Strange growths appear on the leaves and stems of plants.

What do gall wasps do?

They may look like brown apples, little porcupines, bits of moss. Many of these are made by gall wasps. The female pokes her eggs into the plant, which then forms the gall. Just how it forms is not fully understood. The larvae feed on the material inside the home that the plant has helpfully made. Often they spend the entire winter in this shelter. Each kind of insect produces a definite kind of plant gall.

None of the wasps in this chapter are true social insects. But a few wasps live in families, like their cousins the bees. Most of them make their homes in paper nests.

The next chapter will describe what takes place inside the walls of these paper palaces.

Some typical insect galls — swollen plant tissue — caused by the hatching of wasp eggs.

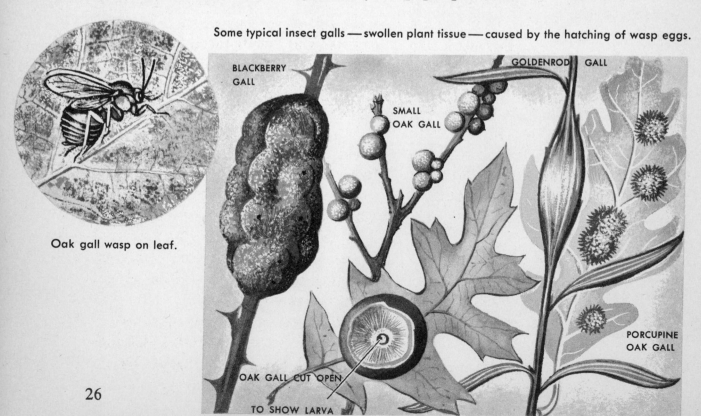

Oak gall wasp on leaf.

BLACKBERRY GALL

GOLDENROD GALL

SMALL OAK GALL

OAK GALL CUT OPEN TO SHOW LARVA

PORCUPINE OAK GALL

HEAD OF POLISTES WASP
(ENLARGED)

The Paper Palace

HEAD OF BALD-FACED HORNET
(ENLARGED)

How long ago was the first paper made?

When was paper originally made? Was it over five hundred years ago, when Johann Gutenberg printed a Bible in 1455? Two thousand years ago, when the Chinese made paper from mulberry bark? Four thousand years ago, when the Egyptians wrote on flat sheets from the papyrus reed? The truth is that paper was first made *millions* of years ago. No human hand touched that first sheet of paper. It was probably manufactured in much the same way as it is today — by a queen wasp, making a shelter for her eggs and larvae.

She goes to a piece of dried wood on a tree or the side of a

How do wasps make paper? house. Her strong little jaws work like scissors. She cuts chunks of wood and mixes them with her saliva. Getting all she can carry, she sometimes tucks extra pieces "under her chin" between her head and first pair of legs. Then she flies back to her home, chewing on the pieces. When she spreads out the mixture, it dries to a tough paper.

It is a mystery how she determines where she will place

Where can wasp nests be found? her new home. Often it is on the end of a tree branch or under the roof of a house. But sometimes she chooses strange places. One wasp nest was built high on a factory chimney, next to the whistle. Everytime the whistle blew, hundreds of wasps buzzed in all directions. Another nest was made in a car that had been in a used-car lot all summer. Still another was built over a schoolhouse door. School couldn't be opened in September until the wasp nest was removed from its unusual location.

What is the difference between a wasp and a hornet? Hornets

What is a hornet? are short, active wasps that live by the hundreds in their paper nest. "Yellowjackets" and "white-faced hornets" are actually special kinds of wasps.

Just like the bees, there are workers, drones and queens. But most wasp paper palaces last only a few months. On the other hand, a beehive may last for years.

The queen chews the wood until it makes a sticky paste. Then she plasters it on the underside of a branch or roof or the interior of an animal's den. Even a family of skunks has to move out when the wasps move in.

She makes a little six-sided paper cell. It is shallow at first and hangs downward. She places a single egg in

A Polistes queen scrapes wood to make paper.

The first room of a Polistes' home looks upside down. It is a cuplike cell attached to a paper stem. As soon as it is completed, an egg is "cemented" into it.

the cell, covered with a sticky material so it won't fall out. A few more cells and eggs complete her little nest.

When the larvae hatch out, they are

How do baby wasps live?

legless and blind like the bee larvae. Often they have sticky "glue pads" on them to hold them in their upside-down cradle. Their mother catches flies and other insects to feed them. She chews up the insects into a little ball. Then she holds the ball down where the babies can feed on it. She puts it first into one cell and then another until it is all gone. Each larva has a few bites. Then the mother flies away for more insect food with which to feed her larvae.

As her larvae get bigger, she keeps adding to the length of the cells. Finally, her half-dozen youngsters emerge as adult wasps. Sometimes the mother is killed before they complete their growth. Then a little empty wasp nest is all that remains to show where she had started housekeeping.

The new wasps help their mother. They

How do the new wasps help in the nest?

build more cells until they have a big, flat layer of them. Then they add a second layer below that, separated from the "floor" above. There may be a dozen layers in the completed nests, each layer having several hundred cells. When they are filled with larvae, and the workers are hunting for food, all the insects around the nest are in danger.

Sometimes a cow in a pasture will walk close to a hornet nest. As she goes slowly by, eating the grass, the hornets discover the flies buzzing around her. One by one they pick them off, never hurting the cow at all. In fact, the cow doesn't even seem to notice them.

As the nest gets larger, the workers build a paper bag around it. This may be of many layers and it serves as insulation. It keeps out noontime heat and the cold of evening. It also serves as a "raincoat" for the nest. Sometimes, if the wood came from a painted building, it may be streaked with colors. Some

Strange-looking larvae, hanging upside down, hatch from the Polistes' eggs. They are fed with chewed caterpillars (above). At right, the finished "paper palace"; a Polistes' nest, showing many chambers, and adult wasps.

paper wasps may build nests three or four feet across, containing thousands of insects.

There is one question which still puzzles scientists. Honey-

How are queen wasps produced?

bees feed royal jelly to a larva to produce a queen, but how are queen wasps produced? They are not grown in oversize cells, nor are they given special food. Yet a large colony may have several queens, all getting along together and all laying eggs in the empty cells.

Some scientists think they may have the answer. Wasps lick each other, just as the other social insects do. Perhaps some special material from an egg-

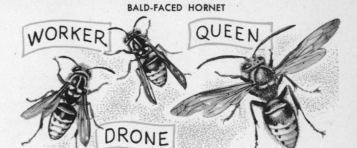

BALD-FACED HORNET

WORKER   QUEEN   DRONE

Hornets' nest with some adult insects.

YELLOW JACKET

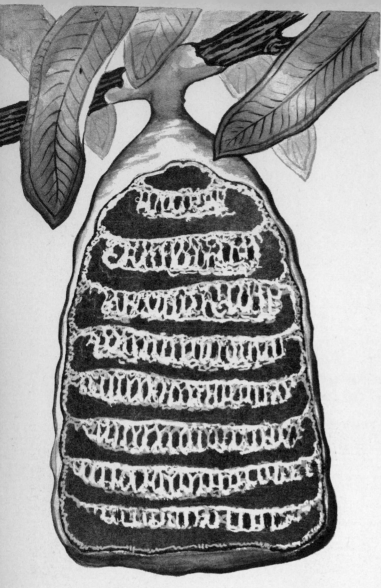

Cutaway view of the nest of a tropical wasp.

her own, so no more queens will grow until the hive is much larger. But this has not been proved.

Autumn is approaching. The queens are not laying so

What happens to the wasps in the fall?

many eggs. Some of them are laid without being fertilized by the male sperm, which the queens have stored in their bodies. These turn into drones. Like drone bees, they cannot sting. They visit flowers and ripened fruit, drinking the sweet liquids. As with the drone bees, they are waiting for the coming of new queens.

Now more queens hatch out. They fly into the air and mate with the drones. They circle around the nest for a while and then leave their paper palace. The workers, too, spend more time flying around and less time in feeding the babies.

People in the country ask in the fall, "Where are all the wasps coming from?" Of course, they have been in their nests all along, but now they are no longer doing their household duties. Their days in the sun will be cut short with the first frost. Then they will fall lifeless to earth. Only the new queens will remain — safely hidden under a bit of bark — to start a new paper palace in the spring.

laying queen is passed around in the licking process. This prevents other wasps from laying eggs by acting on their systems in some way. But when a nest gets too large, only a little bit of the queen's material goes to each worker. Finally one is able to lay eggs. Now she begins to produce material of

ANTS

We have learned that there are species of wasps and bees that do not live in societies, but are solitary insects. There are, however, no solitary ants. Even the most primitive kinds are organized into communities, and the ants are the most highly developed species of the insect world.

Like the bees and wasps that live in communities, the ants have classes, or castes, among the adults. Like bees, the workers are females, mostly unable to lay eggs, but their occupations are more numerous than those in the bee society. The worker is usually much smaller than the queen and has no wings. Ant queens and males have wings which they use in their mating flight and while searching for new colony sites.

The Forest of Grass

When do the winged ants fly? Day after day the hundreds of large new queens and little drones have made their way toward the entrance to the ant hill. But each time something seemed to stop them. Sometimes it would be a mass of workers dragging in a dead

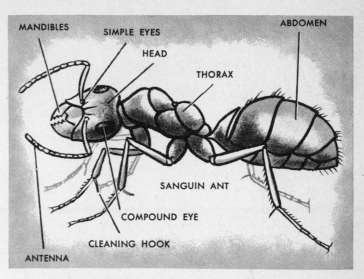

An ant looks like three insects pinned together.

Sanguin ants use their antennae to communicate.

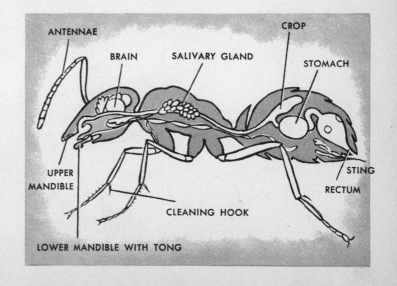

Cross section through a sanguin ant's body. The crop, located in the abdomen just in front of the stomach, is actually a second stomach and one of the most unusual parts of the ant's anatomy. All food is first collected in this crop. From here, the ant presses food back in her mouth to feed the queen or the other ants that have stayed at home. If the ant needs nourishment herself, she has to press food from the crop into her own stomach. The cleaning hooks on the front legs are used exclusively for cleaning of the antennae. Clean antennae provide "good reception."

beetle. Sometimes the workers themselves would bar the way. But today, with the sun shining on the summer meadows, it is different.

Like the swarming bees or the paperwasps in the fall, the ants lay aside their daily work. Workers and soldiers rush back and forth. They wave their antennae and push each other. Sometimes a huge soldier picks up a little worker and carries her around for half an hour. In the middle of it all the queens and drones flutter their untried wings.

The activity spills outside the nest, like boiling water from a kettle. One after the other the winged ones climb up sticks and blades of grass. They stretch their new wings for a moment — and are gone. Up into the air they go, until they are tiny points of light in the sunshine. They have left the nest forever. The wingless workers that have followed them to the tips of the grass blades now turn back toward the ant hill below.

Who are their enemies? All around are the chattering birds. Robber flies and dragonflies dart back and forth. Spiders find their webs filled with dozens of new victims. The whole meadow is filled with activity, for hundreds of nests have sent out their little aviators at once. Now the birds and other creatures are having a feast.

A heavy-bodied queen has flown above the trees at the edge of the field. She meets a drone one-third her size. They mate in the air. Then, like the drone bee, the male flutters dying to the ground.

The new queen glides to a landing. **What does the queen do with her wings?** Then she does an astounding thing. Hooking her legs up over those shiny wings, she twists the wings until they break off.

One after the other, the wings fall to

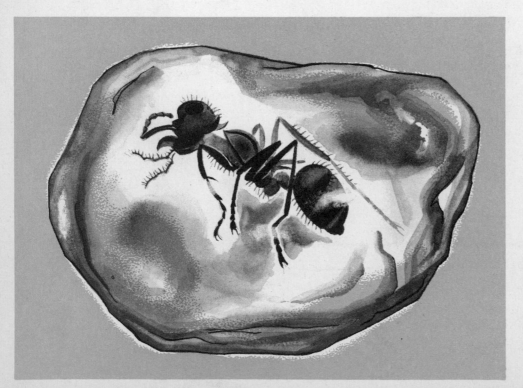

Most animals changed considerably in the course of millions of years of the earth's history. Many became extinct. But the ants have survived and changed only little, as is apparent from this early specimen, trapped and preserved in resin millions of years ago.

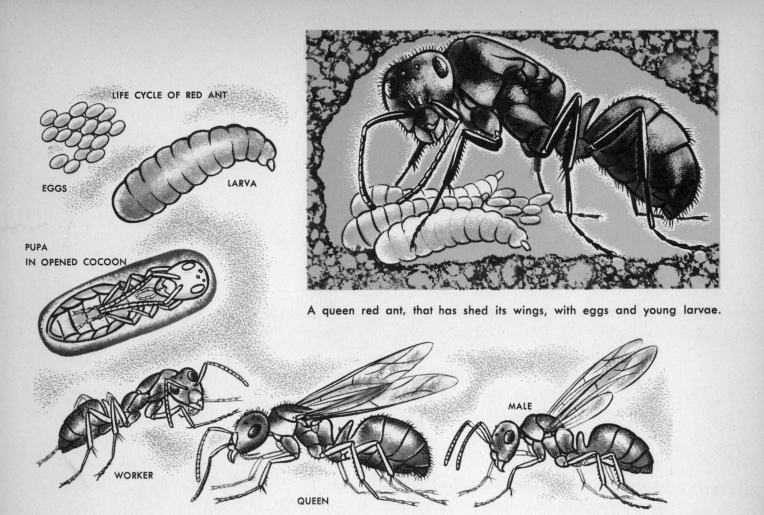

LIFE CYCLE OF RED ANT

EGGS

LARVA

PUPA
IN OPENED COCOON

A queen red ant, that has shed its wings, with eggs and young larvae.

WORKER

QUEEN

MALE

earth. Now she looks strange and hump-backed. Her huge muscles no longer have any wings to operate. But they will soon have another job to do.

She hunts quickly for a place to hide. Burrowing under a stone, she digs into the earth. There she makes a little chamber and seals it tight. Alone in the dark, she begins her new family.

Here is where her great wing-muscles are put to work again. They begin to shrink, giving their nourishment back to her body. As she absorbs their strength, she lays half a dozen eggs. In a day or two a few more are produced. Finally she has a little cluster of eggs.

Sealed in her chamber, how can she find any food? There are no workers to help her gather insects or crumbs. When the first larvae hatch in a few days, what will there be for them to eat?

But food is near at hand. Strange as it seems, the queen **What do the new larvae eat?** picks out an egg and feeds it to a newly-hatched larva, then another egg to another larva, and so on. The little babies, half-starved on such a limited diet, can hardly survive. She gives them saliva from her mouth, but they are still so tiny that it seems they will shortly die.

Finally, they form little cocoons. Some of them starve before **What are "minims"?** they emerge. At last, perhaps a month or two after the first egg was laid, a single worker comes out. She is joined by three or four more. Called "minims" because of their tiny size, they are the only hope for a new ant colony. Their mother's strength is nearly gone. They break through the walls of the chamber. Out in the sunshine, they find the food that is so badly needed. Carrying it back, they give it to their mother.

When she is stronger, she lays more eggs.

What kind of nests do ants build?

The larvae are cared for by the little workers, and they continue to grow bigger and stronger. When they turn into workers themselves, they may be twice as large as their older sisters. They may live six months or more — far longer than the little minims. Then they take care of still bigger and stronger larvae. A nursery is hollowed out for the brood of larvae. Carpenter ants cut galleries in wood. Meadow ants make their homes under the earth. Woodland ants build huge ant hills of sticks and soil. Each kind of ant builds its special home.

Ant hills are more than just piles of dirt thrown out by the ants. They are filled with tunnels and passageways. As the sun hits the hill, the nurses bring the larvae up into the warm soil. If it gets too hot, they are moved over to the shaded side. If it is too cold, they are brought nearer the surface.

Around the home of the ant is a forest

How do ants find their way?

of grass. Each leaf and stone is a part of her world. Scientists think she can recognize them by sight. She goes out in the "forest" each day to find food for her colony. She finds her way by following the scent left by her sisters. She may use the same trail for long distances, sometimes a hundred feet or more, and she may travel it for five or six years. Ants have the longest life span of any insects.

Often they keep their little grass forest as clean as a city park. Each day they carry away bits of food that have been left behind. They toss aside sticks and pebbles. They sweep the ground with their front feet. They even cut the grass near the nest entrance, like gardeners mowing a lawn.

Down beneath the surface, the nest

How do ant larvae live?

is always active. The little larvae are shaped like the letter "j." They are carried from one nursery to another by the workers. Sometimes a worker carries six or eight of them at once. Their sticky bodies cling together. She puts them on a piece of food, leaving them to eat like little sheep put out to pasture. Then she may walk right on top of them as she goes back for more.

HARVESTER ANT WITH SEED

LITTLE BLACK ANTS

EGGS

LARVAE

Finally, after several days, the ant larvae spin tiny cocoons. A few of them are larger than the others, while a few more are smaller. Within these special cocoons a wonderful thing is happening. The pupae are growing their own magic carpets — four shining wings which will carry their owners far above the nest.

Of all the thousands of ants in the ant hill, only these few special ones can enjoy the freedom of flight. They are the new queens and drones.

Some queen ants live for sixteen or **How long do queen ants live?** eighteen years. They may move every few weeks, like the army ants, or they may spend years in the same nest. But even the most stay-at-home ants may move to a new spot. What decides when and where they will move? This is just one of the questions about ants that still waits for an answer.

What do ants eat? While bees eat only nectar and pollen, ants eat many things. They eat nectar if they can get it, but pollen is too hard for their taste. They eat insects and the sweet juices of fruit. Seeds of grasses and berries are also a part of their diet.

How do ants tell others about food? When an ant comes across a large supply of food, it rushes back to the nest. Waving its antennae and striking with its feet, it whacks every ant in its path. It pushes them away from whatever they are doing. Such unusual behavior sets them to doing the same thing, until they are all jostling and shoving. Sometimes they even butt each other with their heads, like little goats. Soon the nest looks as if it were a free-for-all fight.

Now they begin to spill out of the nest, still pushing and shoving. They run around in little circles and zigzag lines. Sooner or later a few find the food. Then the pushing starts all over again as soon as they get back home. This may keep up until the food is gone.

Sometimes several ants find a chunk of food at once, and try to bring it back to the nest. Most of them pull in the right direction, but a few do not. They tug north while the rest tug south. Some even get on top and tug upward!

FIRE ANT

ARMY ANT

CARPENTER ANT

ECITON ANT

PHARAOH'S ANT

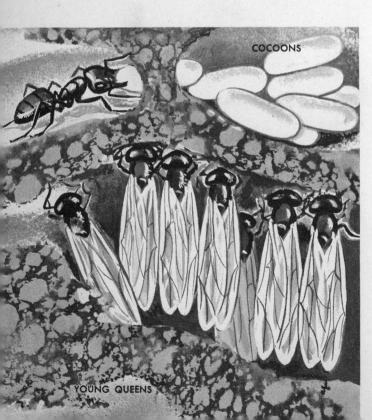

COCOONS

YOUNG QUEENS

Ants usually keep their young of different ages in different rooms. Here is a formica ants' nest with a group of winged young queens, eggs, cocoons and larvae, all separated and cared for by workers.

The army ants are nomadic and have no permanent nests. They move in large columns, carrying along eggs, larvae and cocoons.

Army ant workers, a third the size of "royalty," attend a queen.

Armies on the March

Something is happening in the forest.

How do the army ants live?

There is a soft rustling sound on the forest floor. It is almost like the falling of distant rain. The jungle animals are behaving strangely. At the edge of a clearing, mice and lizards run ahead — and then stop. Then they run again.

Several birds are flying over a dark, soft-looking carpet, catching insects that leap into the air. The "carpet" moves slowly ahead.

An army of ants is on the march. Hundreds of thousands of workers cut and slice at everything that moves.

Coming across a grasshopper, they force it to jump. But it may jump in the wrong direction and land right in the middle of them. They quickly cut it in pieces. Then they send the chunks back toward the end of the line where the larvae are waiting to be fed. This is the family without a home, the gypsy band of the tropics. Even jungle cats and huge snakes flee from the fierce attack of these ants.

Somewhere in the rear of the army is the queen. Like the queen honeybee, she is a prisoner, although there are no walls around her. She is so heavy with eggs that she would be helpless by her-

ARGENTINE ANT

CORNFIELD ANT

A fierce little army ant attacks a much larger tarantula, and usually wins the fight.

self. As fast as she lays eggs, they are taken away by nurse ants and cared for during the first few weeks. Larvae are hatched from these eggs. Then the larvae form pupae. Soon ants emerge as quick-running workers or huge soldiers with jaws so heavy that they cannot feed themselves.

Army ants live in the African and South American tropics. Sometimes their lines may be several hundred feet long. They are often made of two streams. One stream carries food back to the nursery, while the other is going out for more. They even climb to wasp nests and attack the grubs in their paper cells. The wasps are completely helpless against such huge numbers of ferocious enemy ants.

How many kinds of ants are known? There are about fifteen thousand species of ants known. Like the army ants, most of them hunt and wage war, although they are not so easily seen. From the tiny, yellow, kitchen "grease ant," so small that it can hide under a grain of sugar, to the huge Brazilian Ponerine ant that is over an inch long, they live from one battle to the next. Even those that do not catch other insects for food have to defend their nests against many enemies.

Sometimes hunting ants bring back

What ants have slaves? other ant pupae to be slaves. After these emerge, they take care of their new stepbrothers and sisters as if they were their own family. They may even go into battle against members of their old nest, but they are raised to take over much of the work in the nest for their masters.

CARPENTER
ANT
IN WOOD

FIRE ANT

Sometimes farmers use hunting ants as

How are some ants useful? insect traps. In the tropics, some of them live in logs or hollow vines. The farmer places the nest in an orchard tree. The hunters clean out every insect. Then the farmer moves the nest to another tree, or makes a "bridge" of sticks for the ants to cross from one tree to another. Soon a whole section of orchard is free of insects.

Some ants are farmers themselves. The

What are ant farmers? leafcutting ants of South and Central America raise mushrooms for food. They snip pieces of leaves from trees and bushes and carry them along over their heads like little umbrellas. Back at the nest, they bury them deep underground. Soon a special fungus grows on them that the ants use for food. When a queen ant starts a new home, she takes a bit of this fungus with her.

"Go to the ant, thou sluggard," said King Solomon in the Bible. "Consider her ways and be wise." He was probably thinking of another ant farmer, the harvester. When the seeds are ripe, the harvesters carry them to the nest. Long lines of ants can be seen in the Middle East, each ant carrying a seed.

Then the ants set up a "chewing society." Hour after hour they chew on the seeds. Chemicals in their saliva help change the starch of the seeds to sugar. Then this "ant bread" is fed to the larvae.

Many ants eat the sweet substance

How do ants keep "cows"? called "honeydew." It comes from aphids or plant lice as they feed on the sap of plants. The ant strokes

This cross section through the nest of the garden ants shows the mound of earth thrown up by the insects. Passages lead deep into the ground where the real nest lies.

38

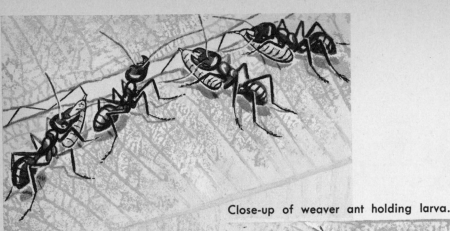

Close-up of weaver ant holding larva.

Above, some weaver ants hold two leaves, while behind the leaves other ants, holding larvae which secrete a thread, "stitch" the leaves together to build their nest.

Finished nest of the weaver ant, built from leaves woven together.

the aphid almost as if it were a farmer milking a cow. The aphid gives out a little drop of honeydew. Sometimes the ants will even pick up the aphids in their jaws and carry them to a new spot. Other times, if the honeydew is not coming fast enough, the ant may go ahead and eat the whole aphid.

In the southwestern United States the

What are honey ants? strange honey ants have their living storage jars. They go out to search for the nectar from flowers. Coming back to the nest, they give the nectar to a young ant, called a "callow," whose body is still soft and flexible. She hangs by her hind legs from the roof of a little underground room. Larger and larger she gets, until she is round and clear, like a little yellow marble. Then she serves as a storage jar for her sisters. Sometimes she hangs there as long as three years — sometimes shorter. If the honey ants give the callow too much nectar, she bursts.

Little underground gardens, aphid "cows" and living honeypots attract

How do ants protect their nests? enemies. But the workers have many ways of fighting them. Although workers cannot fly, the "bulldog" ants of Australia can jump. Sometimes they leap a foot into the air. Many ants have fiery stings. Some bite with their jaws and then spray a burning fluid from their bodies into the wound. Some even use little "squirt guns." Pointing the end of their bodies upward, they squirt out a drop of liquid.

Ant hills may be eight feet high. The

How large are ant hills? "gardens" of the fungus-growing leafcutters may be seven feet beneath the surface. But the largest families and the largest homes do not belong to the ants at all. They belong to the termites, sometimes wrongly called "white ants." Their story will be told in the next chapter.

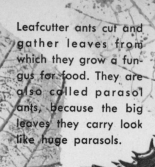

Leafcutter ants cut and gather leaves from which they grow a fungus for food. They are also called parasol ants, because the big leaves they carry look like huge parasols.

The fragments of the leaves are chewed up in the nest and mixed with saliva for the "garden." But leafcutter ants do not feed on the leaves.

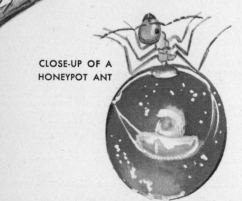

CLOSE-UP OF A HONEYPOT ANT

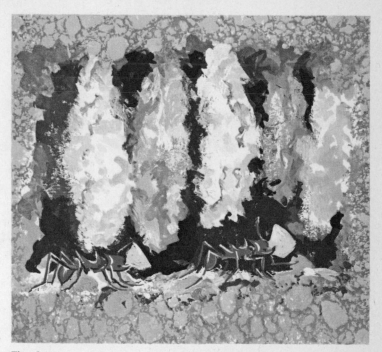

The fungus garden is a sponge-like mass that is full of passages. It is situated in a special chamber of the nest, far under the ground.

The desert ant uses some members of the colony as storage containers, filled to the bursting point with sweet juices. They are hung up in specially constructed chambers. During the lean months, when the galls on which desert ants normally feed do not provide a regular diet, the ants feed from their honey-juice "storage containers."

Ants stroke aphids, little plant lice, with their antennae and squeeze a drop of honeydew out of their abdomens — like farmers milking cows.

TERMITES

The Wooden Cavern

The newborn termite struggles with a piece of wood.

What are newborn termites like?

The chunk, chewed off by a worker a few minutes before, is twice the baby's size. But the baby moves the wood from the center of the dark tunnel. Then it goes along to find another job. In the termite nest, even the babies go to work.

Unlike the larvae of the bees, wasps and ants, the young termite can get around all by itself. It trots around on its six legs, not needing a nursery or a protecting cell. Called a *nymph*, it looks like a miniature copy of the adults all around it.

At first it needs special food. It stops

What food does it eat?

the older termites which pump up some of the food from their stomachs. Even the males take part in the process, for the male termites work as hard as the females.

As the little termite gets older, its taste for food changes. It begins to gnaw on the sides and walls of its home, which is often hollowed out of wood. It will live on wood and plant material for the rest of its life.

Strange as it seems, the termite cannot

How is a termite's food digested?

digest its own food. Good, unrotted wood must be digested for it. Inside its body

are little creatures called *protozoa*. When the termite sends a load of food down to them, these tiny chemists get to work. They break the wood down into

Termite mounds, especially those in the tropics, are often very high. This one is an African termite mound, taller than the average man.

simpler material — and finally to sugar. Then the termite absorbs the sugar into its own bloodstream. Some kinds of termites live without these tiny helpers, but they do not feed on sound wood. Their food is rotten wood, fungus and decayed material.

TWO TERMITES (ACTUAL SIZE)

The newborn termite has no protozoa in its digestive system. Yet it needs them before it will be able to digest wood. It probably gets protozoa by the "living lollipop" method of licking its neighbors and passing food back and forth. Like all insects, it sheds its skin for growth. At the same time, it loses its protozoa. But after it has licked a few neighbors, the protozoa are back.

Day after day the nymph works in the darkness with thousands of its brothers and sisters. If an accident takes place so that the nest is opened, they quickly seal it up again. Making a paste of saliva and sawdust, they build a new wall. Soon

Why are termite nests closed?

the nest is cool and dark. But it is not the light that disturbs them, for they are blind. The dryness of the outside air would soon kill them, as they need dampness for life.

Termites in houses are careful not to eat right through the wood so that air gets inside their tunnels. This is why it is so hard to know if termites are present. The wood looks the same, whether they are there or not. Only by testing to see if it is solid can one be sure. Sometimes they eat up from the cellar to attic without once breaking out into the open. If they come to a bookshelf, they may eat the shelf and the inside pages of all the books!

The nymph may live six or seven years. If it is going to become a queen or king, little bumps begin to show on its back or thorax. These are the buds of the new wings. If it is just a worker, the bumps never develop. With each shedding of the skin the buds get larger, until the termite reaches its full growth. Then it waits in the nest for the day of flight. Sometimes it may wait six years in desert country.

How long do termites live?

Nobody knows what makes a "flight day" for termites. But suddenly they appear by the thousands. They resemble flying ants, although their waists are thicker and they have equal-sized wings. Ants have thinner waists, and the front wings

What is a termite "flight day"?

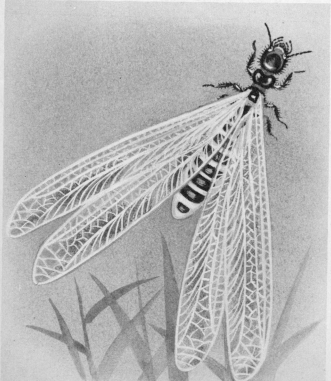

The wings of the termite queen look as if they were made out of a very delicate lace.

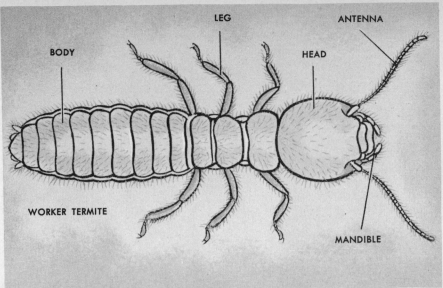

BODY · LEG · HEAD · ANTENNA · MANDIBLE · WORKER TERMITE

Compare this illustration with the one on page 31. It shows why the termite, which is often called the white ant, is as far removed from the white ant as a horse is from a hippopotamus. Their bodies are built differently, the larvae develop differently and the organization of the societies is different. A termite is not a white ant.

are longer than the rear ones. Like ants, they break off the wings when they reach the ground again.

Now a strange thing happens. The female termite raises the tip of her body high into the air. Special scent glands send an odor on the breeze. The wind carries it to a male termite. He cannot fly to meet her, for his wings are broken off, too. So he struggles over sticks and pebbles until he reaches her. Greeting each other by touching their antennae, they find a crack in a log or rotten stump. Then they disappear to mate and start a new home.

How long do royal termites live? Of all the social insects, only the termites have a king. All the other queens are widows, for they have lost their husbands on the mating flight. The termite family gets started very slowly, sometimes with only a few nymphs the first year. But the royal couple is not in a hurry. They are surrounded by food — and they are the longest-lived of all insects. Some scientists believe they may live as long as forty years.

Why is the queen called an egg-machine? The queen gets larger and larger. Her body becomes little more than a huge sack of eggs. They are produced one after another. Soon she is little more than an egg-laying machine. Workers feed her at one end and take the eggs away from the other!

How large are termite houses? The steeple-termite of Africa makes one of the largest insect homes on earth. It may be more than fifteen feet high and built of sand and sawdust mixed with saliva. The royal couple lives inside in its own chamber. The king's egg-filled mate is as big as a sausage. She may lay ten million eggs a year.

What are soldier termites? Perhaps the young nymph is growing up to be a soldier instead of a king, queen or worker. With each molt, its head grows larger and harder. Its jaws get stronger. Soon it seems to be all head. It helps protect the termites against their enemies, the insect-eating ants. If there is a break in the nest, the soldiers rush to that point, their jaws snapping and clicking. They knock their heads against the sides of the galleries. This sets all the termites in motion; soon the hole is repaired.

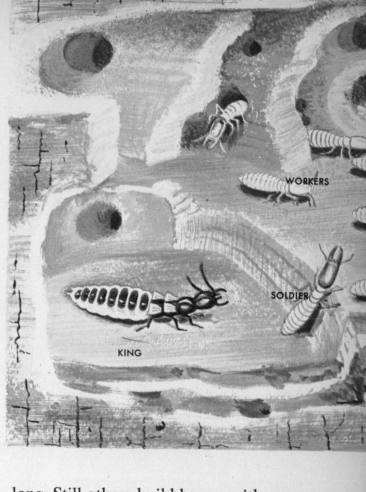

WORKERS

SOLDIER

KING

Some termites have another kind of soldier called a "nasute."

What is a "nasute"? It has a little nozzle on the front of its head. When enemies come, the soldier squirts a messy liquid from the nozzle.

A worker ant, bee or wasp has little chance of ever laying any eggs. But worker or soldier termites sometimes become "second queens." They never get as fat as their huge mother, but they may mate with a male in the nest and start their own egg-factory.

About two thousand species of termites are known.

How many kinds of termites are there? Some of them have their own little fungus gardens on decayed leaves underground, like the gardening ants. Others build homes in trees, with tunnels leading back down to the soil. Some have underground tunnels one hundred fifty feet

KING AND SOLDIER

long. Still others build homes with sawdust umbrellas on top.

But even stranger than the termites are the creatures that live with them, for a termite nest contains odd little guests. So do ant hills, beehives and hornet nests. Some are "beggars" and some are "thieves." The story of insect intruders that force their way into the nests of other insects will be told in the next chapter.

INSECT INTRUDERS

Quietly the little wax-moth makes her way into the beehive.

How can a moth destroy a honeycomb? If the bees find her, they will kill her. The wax-moth lays a few eggs in the hive and flies away.

Soon the eggs hatch. The caterpillars make their way to the comb. They begin to eat the wax, tunneling through it as they go. They leave little silk threads and bits of garbage. Soon the wonderful comb is ruined.

EGGS

QUEEN

The termite "majesties" in the "throne room" of their "castle" (a chewed-up wooden house). The queen is fed by the workers; another worker cares for the eggs; a soldier and the king are standing by. These are wood termites.

Wasp families have their visitors, too.

What insects invade nests of wasps?

Some Vespula wasps of Europe are hard-working paper builders. But a Vespula queen of another species may come along. She enters the nest, fights with the true queen and finally kills her. Soon she is laying her own eggs. After a few weeks, the nest is made up of the new Vespula species.

Wasps sometimes have a little garbage-disposal force. These are the larvae of the common clothes moth. They feed on the empty skins of insects that have been dropped by the wasps. The young of a fly, known as Volucella, feed on dead insects. However, if not enough dead ones are around, the Volucella may quietly eat a wasp grub before the workers can stop it.

Ants have the most guests and visitors.

What is the "paralyzer"?

One bug, called the "paralyzer," has special tufts of hair on its body. The ants lick the secretions from them, but they soon lose control of their muscles. Then the bug feeds on the ants with its pointed beak.

Kidnap-beetles, or rove beetles, hide in the tunnels of ant nests.

What are some other ant visitors?

When a larva is carried past, the beetle snatches it right out of the worker's jaws. Then the beetle races for shelter with its catch. If the ant

A bee comes into the hive with three or

What are some of the other hive-robbers?

four little flies clinging to her. They have no wings of their own. They use the bee like an airplane to take them from place to place. When they get into the hive, they lay their eggs. The tiny larvae eat the wax cap of the bee cradles. When they turn into adult flies, they get aboard another insect airplane.

Sometimes a bee brings in the larva of the oil beetle. This became attached while the bee was visiting a flower for nectar. Now the larva goes crawling to the brood comb. Here it feeds on the bee's eggs before they hatch. Growing larger, the larva steals honey. When it turns into an adult oil beetle, it leaves the beehive.

WINGED MALE AND NYMPH

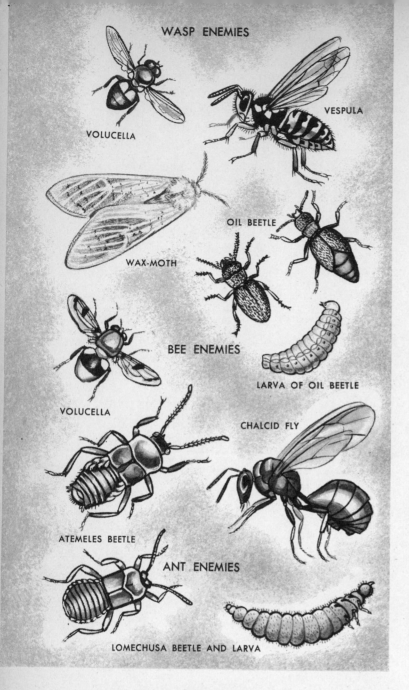

WASP ENEMIES

VOLUCELLA

VESPULA

WAX-MOTH

OIL BEETLE

BEE ENEMIES

LARVA OF OIL BEETLE

VOLUCELLA

CHALCID FLY

ATEMELES BEETLE

ANT ENEMIES

LOMECHUSA BEETLE AND LARVA

way into another ant hill. She snips off the head of the real queen. The ants, without a queen, soon adopt her. They raise her eggs and young. Bit by bit, as the old ants die off, the nest turns into a family of beheading ants.

Some rove beetles seem to have such a pleasant taste that the ants neglect their own brood. They feed and lick the beetles known as Lomechusa. They give them the food that should go to the ant larvae. Meanwhile, the Lomechusa grubs feast on the young ants. After a while the ant hill may die.

Even the blind, dark-loving termites have their little guests. The white mite is a tiny creature. It runs all over the backs and bodies of the termites. When one termite feeds another, the mite is right at hand. It points its beak right into the bubble of food going between them. For some reason the termites don't seem to mind it.

What creatures live in termite homes?

Termite mounds have beetles and bugs of many types. Ants are forever attacking them, too. But two of the termite's worst enemies live right in the walls of the mounds. One is the termite lizard that snaps up every termite it finds. The other is the sun spider or Jerrymunglum. This creature, about three-quarters of an inch long, looks like a brown, hairy spider. Its jaws are like pliers. It forces its way right through the walls of termite tunnels. Then it feeds on the termites.

What is a Jerrymunglum?

chases it, the beetle squirts an unpleasant fluid in the ant's face.

Even the terrible army ants have their camp-followers. Beetles and bugs go along on ant raids. Many of them are shaped like the ants themselves. Probably this keeps them safe from attack. When food is sent back to the queen and the nurses, the camp-followers help themselves. The army ants are blind and probably cannot tell the difference.

The beheading ant queen forces her

Why do social insects allow all these

creatures to live in their nests? Most of them have a taste or odor that the insects seem to like. But this may not be the complete answer.

In the next chapter you will learn how to make your own insect zoo. Then, perhaps, you may find some of the answers yourself.

YOUR INSECT ZOO

Honeybees are fascinating to watch.

How can you watch bees at home?

Perhaps you know of someone who has a hive of his own. A high school biology teacher may be able to help you get an "observation hive." This is a little glass-walled bee colony. Put it in a bright place away from direct sunlight. Then you can watch the bees at work.

What do you feed your captive honeybees? Just leave the window open a half-inch and they will feed themselves. Flying away from their new home, they disappear into the sky. Half an hour later they return, loaded with pollen and nectar.

Wasp nests are best left where you find

How can you watch wasps?

them. But you can still enjoy watching them if you have a pair of binoculars. You will see them bringing flies and other insects.

The underside of roofs and sheltered walls are good places to find mud-dauber wasps. They pay no attention to you if you watch them quietly. Then you will see them bringing spiders to their mud nests. These will serve as food for their newly-hatched larvae.

Sand wasps can be followed as they drag caterpillars along the ground to their holes. Even little plant galls can be brought into the house and kept in a closed jar until the tiny wasps hatch.

An observation ant home is called a

How can you make a nest for ants?

formicarium. It can be made of two panes of glass separated by strips of wood around the edges. Then, if a small ant hill is dug up carefully, you will find the humpbacked queen. Put her in a jar with some of her workers, larvae and cocoons. You will probably discover that you have some of the strange ant guests, too. Carefully place them all in the formicarium.

No soil is needed for your ant nest. Before you seal it up, place a sponge near one edge for moisture. Drill two holes in the wood for two medicine droppers. One is to wet the sponge, and the other is for honey, water and melted butter with a little egg white. This will serve as food for the ants. Then the panes are taped together.

Keep the nest covered with dark paper except when looking at the ants. A piece of red cellophane or glass will

WOOD

TAPE

GLASS

EYE DROPPER

FOOD

WATER

A formicarium with earth between the panes of glass offers a good opportunity to study the interesting life of ants.

let you watch without disturbing them. You will see the ants feeding their queen and caring for their young.

How can termites be kept? If you wish to watch termites, pull apart an old stump or log until you find a family of these insects. Then search carefully for the large king and his larger queen. Put the family in a darkened jar. Add bits of the wood and laboratory filter paper for food. Keep a moist sponge in the jar. There is little danger of your termites getting away, as they would die soon after they left the moisture of the nest.

What is the best insect zoo of all? The best insect zoo, however, is the one that is right outdoors. With a magnifying glass you can watch the insects at work in their own homes. Even a city park has its ants, bees, wasps and termites. A dish of honey on a window sill will soon attract the bees. Mud placed nearby will be found by mud-dauber wasps. Chunks of soft wood will be chewed up by the paper wasps for their homes. A bouquet of flowers in a glass of water will attract insect visitors.

In your outdoor zoo you can watch the ants in their ceaseless battles. You may see other battles, too, for social insects will fight with any insect that is not from their own nest.

You can watch a fighting ant with its abdomen bitten off, still fighting. You can drop a piece of paper on the scent-trail of the ants and watch them try to find the way again. You can learn which colors most attract bees.

There are many other things you can find out yourself. When you see something interesting, write it down. Soon you will have a book of your own.